THE DOVES AND THE MAN WITH THE WHIP OF CORDS

JAN CURCIO

Illustrated by Sue Bloch

WestBow Press books may be ordered through booksellers or by contacting:

WestBow Press
A Division of Thomas Nelson & Zondervan
1663 Liberty Drive
Bloomington, IN 47403
www.westbowpress.com
1 (866) 928-1240

Interior Graphics/Art Credit: Sue Bloch

John 2:16 NKJV

ISBN: 978-1-9736-9221-8 (sc)
ISBN: 978-1-9736-9220-1 (e)

Library of Congress Control Number: 2020909399

Print information available on the last page.

WestBow Press rev. date: 09/10/2020

WESTBOW
PRESS®
A DIVISION OF THOMAS NELSON
& ZONDERVAN

Acknowledgement

To Alex Curcio, whose steadfast
faithfulness has allowed me the
opportunity to write this book

A long time ago in a village outside of the great city of Jerusalem lived a pair of young doves, whose names were Moshe and Bina. They didn't know much about anything other than that they would spend all their days together in their cozy niche and happy dovecote. They had no worries and no cares and enjoyed the company of friends and a kind keeper who cared for them all. But that all came to an end one day when a man came to purchase a dozen doves to be sold at the Temple feast. And after leaving a deposit of a pence for each one, he instructed the keeper to deliver them to his booth at the Temple court on the morning of the feast.

And overhearing all of this, Avi the alpha dove cooed, "Well, it's that time again." "What time?" asked Bina. And with a troubling look on his face, Avi replied, "The time for some of us to be sold for the Temple sacrifice." "What is a Sacrifice?" asked Moshe. "Well, if you have to know," chirped Avi, "I heard our keeper tell his son that an animal must die for someone to be cleansed." "Cleansed, cleansed of what?", asked Yoni, one of the young doves who had been listening to all the chatter. "I can't say," cooed Avi, "But whatever it is, it must be very unclean." And after some thought, Moshe moaned, "There must be a better way, there must be a better way."

And in the following days the doves noticed that their keeper had not been as attentive to them as usual; instead, spending much of his time seated in the garden under the tree next to the dovecote. And covered with a white shawl with blue striping and a tassel on each corner, he could be heard speaking to someone he called LORD. And how curious all of this was to the young doves, who sensed that not all was going to go well for them.

And early one morning, as the sun peeked over the horizon, the keeper and his son came to the dovecote to pick out which doves would go to the Temple market. And as the boy would point to one of them, his father would ask, "That one son?" And if the boy answered, "Yes, Abba," he would take that dove and place it in his wooden cage. And as they passed by Avi's nook, the keeper said with a gleam in his eyes, "Now, you know that we can't take Avi, for he's the daddy of them all." And next to Avi was perched Moshe and Bina not knowing what was about to happen and how it would change their lives forever.

And then the keeper's son pointed to Bina, saying, "That one Abba." "That one, son?" asked his father. And the boy replied, "Yes, that one." And so, the keeper took Bina and put her in the cage with eleven other doves. But it was not without great protest from Moshe, who screeched, "No, no, not her, not my Bina!" And while ignoring his pleas, they went off to the Temple—the father, the son, and the dozen doves.

And back at the dovecote Avi failed to comfort Moshe, who would not stop cooing; as did Bina and her friends all the way to the Temple. And as the father, his son with the twelve doves passed through the arched gates of the great city of Jerusalem, they were met by money changers and sellers of sheep and goats and doves bustling about to prepare for the crowds of worshippers already making their way through the gates.

And after dropping the doves off at the merchant's booth, the keeper and his son returned home to prepare for the feast, only to find Moshe flying frantically about from one end of the dovecote to the other. And not knowing that Moshe intended to escape to rescue Bina, they forgot to close the gate behind them, when Moshe took his chance to flee. And landing for a moment on the roof of the dovecote before flying off on a mission to find Bina, he wondered in which direction he should go.

Moshe only knew that Bina and their friends were taken to the Temple, and while searching below to find it, he wondered just what the Temple would look like. And down below he spotted a great olive tree in a garden on a hill. So being weary from it all, Moshe decided to rest on one of its branches where he noticed many other kinds of birds perched, those he had often seen whizzing by the gate of the dovecote in search of crumbs that might fall from their keeper's pail.

And suddenly a raven swooped down beside Moshe, and asked him, "Where are you going, little dove?" "I'm going to the Temple to find my Bina and eleven friends, where they have taken them away to be sacrificed!" he cooed. "Oh", cackled the raven, "That's not good." And Moshe asked, "What is the sacrifice about?" "Well," answered the raven, "According to a sparrow friend of mine who perches on the Temple, humans come to the feasts from near and afar with sheep and goats and doves to be slaughtered and roasted on the great altar for an offering to their God for the cleansing of their sin. Those who come from far away will buy sheep and goats and doves sold at the Temple. And many of them have been sacrificed over the years." And after some thought, Moshe sorrowfully cooed once again, "But there has to be a better way, there has to be a better way!"

And the raven urged Moshe saying, "You need to get on your way, for they will waste no time in sacrificing them." And as he was about to fly off, Moshe turned and asked the raven, "Tell me, where can I find the Temple?" The raven looked off to the West and said, "See that long line of humans moving towards the hill, they are on their way to the Temple. Follow them." And Moshe turned to him again and asked, "What is your name?" "I am Perez," the raven screeched with pride, "Because I am the best at breaking through!"

And so, Moshe flew down to the long line of humans, landing on the back of a donkey where he could catch his breath and give his weary wings a rest. But soon he was off again climbing higher and higher until he was over the hill where he could see on the other side of the wall of the great city what he thought had to be the Temple.

And gleaming in the rising sun stood the largest and most beautiful house Moshe could have ever imagined. So he asked himself, "But where in all of this is my Bina?" As he landed above the great arched gateway, suddenly a flurry of black feathers descended around him. And to Moshe's surprise it was Perez with three other ravens. "Hey, little dove, you can't do this alone," screeched Perez. "Meet my brothers, Yoshi, Sami, and Gilli. We are going to help you find Bina!"

And led by Perez they lifted off to the pinnacle of the Temple, where they found ten little sparrows nestled along the ledge from where they watched the activity below. "Hey, my friends", cackled Perez, "Tell me where they are selling doves today?" The one Perez knew tweeted back, "They are over there in the far corner of the court in the booths under the porch." And after thanking his little friend, Perez and his brothers and Moshe headed for the roof over the booths of the dove sellers.

And it was from there that they could see the bustling crowds below changing their coins to purchase the sheep and goats and doves for the sacrifice. But Moshe hardly noticed any of the commotion while frantically searching for Bina and their eleven friends. But they had been placed out of site in the back of a booth, all anxiously awaiting what they sensed to be the end of them all. And all Bina could think of was her Moshe, the one she loved more than anyone in the world. And Bina never caught sight of him pacing back and forth on the roof of the porch, stretching his neck to inspect the booths below, landing on the pavement for a moment or two, before returning to the roof for another peek.

Nor did she witness the four ravens on their quest to find her, flying in and out of the booths, ignoring the swats and hisses of the flustered merchants. And while calling out "Bina, Bina, where are you my little dove," Moshe and his new friends became more determined to find her and their friends to set them free. Moshe called out to Bina as loudly as he could to be heard above the bleating sheep and goats and the rushed footsteps of humans crossing the courtyard.

And for a moment Moshe thought that he heard the familiar cooing of Bina below, but could not place it. "I think I hear her, I think I hear her," he shrieked out to Perez and his brothers. And landing on the pavement below, Moshe could hear her cooing more clearly and coming from the direction of the booth before him. But while stepping into the booth, suddenly, he was grabbed from behind by the merchant, the same one who had come to the dovecote days before to pick out a dozen doves. And gleefully the man asked him, "Now, how did you get out of your cage little dove?" And seeing how Moshe looked like the doves he had placed in the back of the booth, he put him in the cage with them, with Bina and their eleven friends.

And while the seller of doves returned to his customers, Perez, Yoshi, Sami, and Gilli flew into his booth undetected, where they found Moshe and Bina and their friends, and began to do what ravens do best—breaking in. But while they picked away at the wooden rungs that held their friends captive, a customer spotted Moshe and Bina, and said to the merchant, "Those two are perfect; I will take them both."

And as the eager merchant took hold of the cage, suddenly there came a great clamor from the courtyard with sounds of shouting and banging and crashing and bleating of sheep and goats that were stampeding in all directions. For they had been set free from their pens by a man swinging a whip of cords, causing great havoc among the stunned merchants. And then there were those angry men in long black robes coming to see what all the commotion was about, who dared not stop the man with the whip of cords from flipping over the money changers' tables and sending coins flying through the air. And turning to the booth of doves, the man with the whip of cords grabbed hold of the cage from the hands of the merchant, and while tearing it open he commanded him, "Take these things away! Do not make My Father's house a house of merchandise!"1

<hr>

1 John 2:16 NKJV

And without hesitation, Moshe, Bina, and their eleven friends were headed for the wall of the city as fast as their wings could take them. And landing above the great arched gateway, they were joined by Perez and his brothers, who led them back to the great olive tree in the garden on the hill east of Jerusalem. And it was in that garden that they remained happy and free all the days of their lives.

And the Temple courtyard would not have been the last place they would see the man with the whip of cords who had set them free. Soon after, that man came with his eleven friends when he knelt under their tree and spoke to his Father, with great drops of blood falling from his face to the ground. But suddenly a mob came and took him away and they never saw him again.

And little did they know that the man with the whip of cords who had set them free would be the one who would make a better way of sacrifice for humankind, who would himself become the sacrifice that would cleanse the sins of those who would believe in Him. And they never heard that His name was Jesus of Nazareth, who is the Son of God, the Creator of all that exists, who came to dwell among humankind because he loved them, and that he would be returning someday to take with Him those who love Him.

Printed in the United States
By Bookmasters